Introduction

Your first look at a large iguana will probably make you recall a cheap monster movie of the Godzilla variety, where lizards with taped-on spines and shields lumber through miniature cities with close-up photography attempting to make it believable. Iguanas have, in fact, starred in some of these productions and, with their vivid colors, stripes, spines and claws, needed very little make-up to get the parts!

You can also grow a bit nostalgic when looking at an iguana for they make it so

A "rhinoceros" iguana, a variety with pointed scales ("horns") on the snout. This may be more a factor of growth than genetics, and the condition does not represent a separate species.

easy to imagine the Great Age of Reptiles, which has come and gone, leaving not one single dinosaur alive, but museums full of bones, footprints, and these smaller descendants for us to study and enjoy.

A BRIEF LESSON IN TAXONOMY

Although we use the term "iguana" as if it designates one particular lizard, the iguana family is a large and varied group of lizards tied together by several anatomical similarities. The family Iguanidae is one of approximately seventeen lizard groups recognized by taxonomists as being distinctly different from each other to warrant individual families. Within each family are several genera (a genus is a group of similar and related species). In turn, each genus may encompass several different species (a species is a group of animals that look alike and can breed together to produce similar-appearing offspring). Our

Iguana delicatissima, the Antillean Iguana, is a full species from the lower Caribbean islands that lacks the enlarged scales at the angle of the lower jaw found in the true or Common Iguana.

Adult Common Iguanas like the one on this and the facing page have a crest of high spines, enlarged circular scales at the back angle of the lower jaw, and usually have some broken dark bands over the body.

pet Green Iguana, or Common Iguana as it is often called, bears the distinction of not only being an iguanid (a member of the iguana family) but belonging to the genus *Iguana* and the species *iguana* also. With *Iguana iguana* beings its official, if redundant, title, most people

about thirty eggs. Iguanas are indigenous to tropical America and are a very common reptile throughout Central and South America. Iguanids as a family are considered a New World group because, with very few exceptions, they are confined to the Americas

simply accept the name "iguana" to describe this beast.

The iguana begins its life as an inconspicuous little hatchling wriggling from an egg in early spring. About two-thirds of its eight-inch body will be tail, and although it will resemble its parents in miniature, there will be nothing about this little creature to make you suspect that it will one day become a six-foot-long giant. Iguanas are quite prolific in the wild and our pet hatched from an average clutch of

and surrounding areas. Although other like-appearing long green lizards occur in the other parts of the world, they possess structural differences great enough to place them not only in a different genus and species but in different families. In Asia, for example, we find an iguana look-alike called the Chinese Water Dragon (*Physignathus cocincinus*) which also finds its way into the pet trade on occasion. So striking is the resemblance between this large green lizard and our

Green Iguana that, on more than one occasion, the author has seen color photographs of these lizards in herpetological texts mislabeled with the genus and species of the impostor! Scientists refer to this phenomenon as convergent or parallel evolution, the

think of a lizard such as the tiny anole (*Anolis carolinensis*, the American Chameleon) as a closer relative to the huge iguana than an Asian lizard which looks nearly identical, the fact remains that taxonomists must use precise criteria such as tooth placement, skull formation

situation occurring when two animals from different families in different parts of the world evolve to reach amazingly similar results. Despite the nearly identical appearance of the Water Dragon and the Green Iguana, a number of minute differences such as tooth placement (acrodont in the Water Dragon versus pleurodont in the Green Iguana) subsume the Water Dragon into the Old World (Africa, Asia, etc.) family Agamidae. While it may be confusing to the layman to

and scale counts to discern differences in lizards and often must disregard the coincidence that some look alike and others do not.

THE IGUANA IN CAPTIVITY

Iguanas have enjoyed much popularity in recent years for a number of good reasons. Even though there are many beautiful lizards available on the pet market, an adult iguana, with its vivid green and blue coloration, striped tail and long dorsal spines, can hold a candle to any of them. The animal is common enough in the wild to supply the ever-growing pet trade without (hopefully) diminishing the wild population to any great extent, and this availability has kept it a very affordable pet to purchase. Although the iguana's heat, light and dietary needs may seem tedious to the average dog and cat owner, most hobbyists consider it a very hardy species and much easier to care for than most other reptiles. The iguana's habit of eating from a bowl, as a dog or cat would, appeals to a lot of people who normally would shy away from reptiles because of their usual need for live food, such as crickets and small rodents. The overall size attained by an adult iguana is what first intrigues many people, although it is probably the longevity of the animal that ultimately astonishes newcomers. A well-cared-for iguana can easily pass the ten-year mark in captivity, with reports of fifteen years becoming more common. Not quite in the league of the hundred-year-old tortoises but certainly rivaling the life span of "man's best friend." Probably the one characteristic of the Green Iguana that pet buyers find most appealing is its reputation for becoming quite tame. Despite the size and obvious strength of a large specimen, an iguana

With few exceptions (usually high-altitude lizards such as some species of horned lizards), iguanids lay eggs that hatch into miniature versions of the parents. These are baby Sceloporus magister, *a western American spiny swift.*

Facing page: Often confused with the Common Iguana is the Asian or Chinese Water Dragon, Physignathus cocincinus. *In addition to belonging to a different family (Agamidae), this species has unique spiny scales at the back of the lower jaw.*

Regular handling makes a young iguana more docile and helps it adapt to captivity better. Don't expect your pet to respond to handling like a cat or dog, however.

should display little or no aggression toward a person if it has been handled regularly throughout its life. Once a new iguana becomes well acclimated to its cage and is eating well, you may want to start handling it on a regular basis, and you should notice its becoming more docile in time. I would not, however, make an issue of taming the iguana nor would I consider it in the best interest of the animal. Many pet owners refuse to accept reptiles for what they are, cold-blooded primitive animals with limited intelligence. When this happens, the pet owner tends to expect human responses from the non-human animal and this anthropomorphism leads to an over-handled, over-stressed pet. On this subject, people will differ sharply on their definition of "pet," but I personally feel that any non-domestic animal given the proper environmental and dietary conditions can make a fine pet and thrive with a minimum of handling. An iguana will never wag its tail when it sees you, come when you call it, or fetch your slipper, but you should not let this lack of response or emotion disappoint you—it makes a beautiful and fascinating pet nonetheless.

A Long Way From Home

Just a few weeks, perhaps months, before you first noticed your new iguana in the pet shop, it was probably lounging comfortably in its homeland of tropical America. A typical setting might be a Brazilian rain forest where our arboreal pet could be found clinging to a tree branch high above a running stream. A well-balanced diet of fruits, flowers, insects and leaves could be reached within a few feet, all free of preservatives and pesticides.

Fresh water from jungle rains would be deposited on leaves and vines frequently, where it could be lapped off, and if startled or threatened, our iguana could leap many feet to the river below and swim to safety. Even more beneficial than these factors would be the constant warming rays of the equatorial sun. Aside from supplying the consistent heat necessary to maintain optimum digestion and metabolism, the intense ultraviolet rays of the tropical sun enable the iguana to perform complex processes within its body and utilize the vitamins in its food to the fullest. It would be hard to picture a more carefree existence than the one in this scenario, where all the ingredients necessary for a perfect life are at arm's length and free for the taking! Paradise? Well, not quite.

Along with being a perfect environment for iguanas, the tropics provide an ideal breeding ground for parasites and harmful bacteria. A plethora of ticks, mites and leeches flourishes here, ready to drain the blood from an iguana and transmit disease in exchange. A variety of predators from large birds to boas (who when hungry may lapse from their "warm-blooded-prey-only" diet) consider iguanas an adequate source of food, especially the unfortunate ones that become weakened or injured. Man cannot be excluded from the list of predators either, as local residents hunt iguanas for

The Common Iguana ranges widely over Central and South America from southern Mexico to Argentina. It usually is found near rivers and lakes and spends almost all its time in the trees. Iguanas are very abundant near this Brazilian riverside cemetery, where they are protected by local superstition. Here they are not very shy and allow close approaches. When badly frightened, they can run over the water for a short distance like a basilisk.

their meat, edible eggs and yes, the inevitable pet trade. With this somewhat more realistic picture of the iguana's homeland in mind, how should we set up a captive environment in which the pet can thrive? Many pet owners feel the need to duplicate the "natural habitat" setting to house their iguanas, creating elaborate terraria with soil, live plants, running water and the like. While undoubtedly picturesque, this well-intended model rain forest is not suitable for a captive iguana for a number of reasons. The

Not all lizards are compatible. Carnivores such as the collared lizards, *Crotaphytus*, will eat smaller lizards caged with them. Consider cagemates for your iguana carefully.

humidity needed to maintain such a terrarium would play havoc with an iguana's health, often causing fungal problems on the animal's skin. Any soil, moss or humus would harbor too many germs and bacteria, and if your live plants were to flourish, the iguana would probably just eat them anyway! Select instead a simple dry terrarium and keep it as basic as possible; what you may lose in appearance, you will gain in the health of your pet.

A NEW HOME

Although a number of different types of cages can be purchased or constructed, the most common choice is a standard glass fish aquarium. It is extremely easy to clean and maintain, offers unobstructed visibility, and is much easier to heat than a screen or wood enclosure. A twenty- to thirty-gallon size will probably suffice for the first year or two, although you may want to anticipate your iguana's future size and start second. Points to keep in mind are: 1.) moisture/odor control, 2.) cleanliness, 3.) ease in maintenance, 4.) heat conduction, 5.) cost and 6.) appearance. I'll try to cover each of the several common choices categorically and point out what I've found to be the benefits and drawbacks.

Although dominant males may fight at first, you can cage several iguanas together in a large cage with few incidents. Watch to make sure that all are allowed to eat, however, and that fights do not get serious.

with a larger (forty- to one-hundred-gallon) model. You will have to decide what to use for a substrate (bottom lining) in the cage and there are several possibilities from which to choose. Once again the most attractive choice may not be the most practical one, and we should always consider the pet's health first and the terrarium's appearance

Paper toweling/Brown paper: A good sterile substrate, ideal for quarantine cage (new or injured specimens). Moderately expensive considering that it should be replaced daily. Obviously lacking in appearance but very functional.

Sand: The fine white silica sand available in pet shops is one of my personal favorites.

Water Dragons are now widely available and often easier to find than Common Iguanas. They require water in which to swim and will eat more animal protein than Common Iguanas but are somewhat similar otherwise. Young specimens of both Water Dragons and Common Iguanas may be heavily infested with worms in the intestinal tract.

It offers excellent heat dissipation; a good "heatrock" partially buried in dry sand should make for quite a warm cage floor. Overall appearance is pleasing and it offers good light reflection, making for a bright cage. Stray food and feces dehydrate quickly and can be scooped out "kitty-litter" style, keeping moisture and odor to a minimum. Should the sand become saturated (i.e., water-dish spillage), it should be removed and spread on trays to dry or be baked in an oven. Young iguanas that constantly dive for crickets and mealworms may consume too much of this substrate or receive mouth abrasions, so it is recommended with this qualification in mind.

Depending on the size of your pet, this substrate need only be replaced every month or so (when odor starts to build up) and the cost is reasonable.

Gravel: Similar to sand in most respects, slightly more expensive but it can be washed, rinsed and dried so it should last indefinitely. Although some other publications indicate that an iguana may willfully ingest gravel to aid digestion processes (like a bird's crop), I have never witnessed my own iguanas consuming gravel voluntarily (i.e., parakeet grit offered in a separate dish), but confirmed cricket-divers will have moderate amounts in their feces when it is used as a substrate.

Ground corncob/Wood shavings: These two substrates are borrowed from the world of exotic-bird care, where they are commonly used for cage lining. Virtually unbeatable for moisture absorption and odor control, they haven't caught on with the reptile crowd due to their lack of visual appeal. Cost is low despite the fact that these substrates should be replaced every few days, and nearly the only practical drawback I've found is poor heat conduction. In fact, I would not trust any sort of "heat rock"' heating fixture buried in one of these flammable substances and a cage lined with either of these should be heated externally.

Wood chips: Available at greenhouses and plant nurseries, wood chips make an excellent cage flooring. Advantages are similar to wood shavings, only the appearance is more attractive and natural. Select only dry, clean chips, usually sold in bulk as "redwood chips" rather than the pre-bagged kind which may contain a lot of moisture. Also, selecting large enough chips will prevent ingestion by the lizards. Cost is very low; disadvantages are poor heat dissipation, flammability,

and the likelihood of crickets, which seem to be able to hide forever in this stuff.

Artificial grass: Last and probably best is the green indoor-outdoor carpeting sold as patio or porch covering. Combining ease in maintenance with nice appearance, this is an excellent choice, especially for the beginning hobbyist. While not especially absorbent, moisture will dissipate quickly on this synthetic material and odor/

Hot rocks, heating blocks of plaster or similar material, may be provided to basking iguanas but are not without their dangers. Because iguanas sense heat from above more than below, there is a possibility that bad stomach burns could result from staying on a hot rock too long. This has been known to kill some lizards. Use caution with hot rocks.

bacteria build-up is minimal. A thorough washing should be done weekly and takes only minutes, plus a half hour or so to dry. Heating rocks can be used safely on it and crickets are easy to catch on the surface.

HEATING THE CAGE

Iguanas are from the tropical regions of South America and require very high temperatures. By no means can we expect an iguana to thrive at "room temperature," it simply cannot be done without serious risks to the animal's well-being. Try to shoot for average temperatures of 90–95°F within the cage, with lows of 80° and highs of 105°F being the critical limits. Have an accurate thermometer in the cage and follow it religiously—do not try to cut corners in this area. One way to heat the cage is simply to heat the room around it. Although this may be impractical for keeping only one pet, if you plan to keep several iguanas or a variety of specimens, designating a "reptile room" and heating it to a high ambient temperature might be the easiest solution. If this is not desirable, you will have to heat the tank itself and there are a number of ways to accomplish this. A heating pad or water-bed heater does a good job and can be used in a variety of ways. Externally a pad can be taped to the bottom or back wall of an aquarium and will radiate quite a bit of warmth by heating that

perch. A few words should be said here about placement of the heat source in regard to the appearance of the cage. Although heat sources, such as pads or heat rocks which lay at the bottom of the cage, are the most commonly used, they will draw the iguana to the floor of the cage, contrary to the animal's arboreal habits and creating an unnatural viewing condition. One expects to see an iguana perched atop a branch or driftwood log, not sprawling

Both light and heat are essential provisions for the proper care of iguanas. Some companies produce bulbs that furnish both these climatic items. Check your local pet shop for such products. Photo courtesy of Energy Savers.

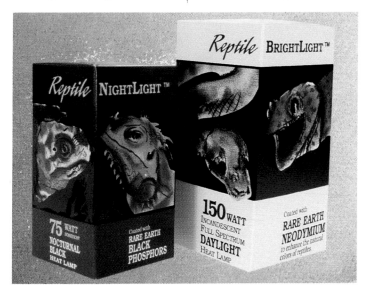

entire pane of glass. Internally a pad can be buried in sand or gravel or hidden under a piece of artificial grass to achieve much the same effect. A more creative approach would be to wrap the pad around a log or branch where the iguana is apt to

on the floor like a lazy dog on a hot summer day!

In this case the scene we desire to see and the one which is healthiest for our pet coincide (for a change), because the iguana seems to prefer a radiant heat source from above, as he would enjoy in the wild. A nice

Bark is a sensible bedding to use with iguanas. It is light in weight and thus easy to work with, relatively inexpensive, and can be bought in quantity. Photo courtesy of Four Paws.

effect is achieved by using a heat source located in the bottom of the cage to supply warmth round the clock and also using a radiant heat source (e.g., light bulb) for daytime basking. This way not only is there a pleasing visual effect obtained but the animal's natural light cycle is imitated also: it will seek the highest points in the cage during the day to be closest to the sun (light bulb) and the floor of the cage at night to lie on objects that store heat (heating pad). Hot rocks, artificial rocks encasing small electric heating units, are popular reptile accessories and are highly recommended. However, I consider them supplementary heat sources only, as most of these will not heat the entire cage. It does your pet little good to lie on a rock with a surface temperature of 100°F while it breathes air at an ambient temperature of 65°F. This

point cannot be stressed enough—iguanas need consistent high temperatures not just a hot spot to warm their bellies. In addition to the fluorescent light with plant-growing bulb that you will be using to illuminate the cage, a basking light as described above is a worthwhile addition. A

Incandescent bulbs (tungsten) can provide heat for an iguana cage, but the bulb must be completely covered to prevent accidents from either breakage or overheating.

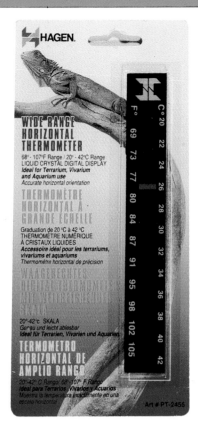

It is very important for a keeper to monitor his or her iguana's ambient temperature, for a temperature that is too high or too low will cause many, many problems. Fortunately, there are high-range thermometers designed specifically for reptile enclosures. Photo courtesy of Hagen.

occur if the animal comes in direct contact with a hot bulb or fixture. Either put the lighting fixture outside the cage (to shine through a screen or glass top) or shield it properly to prevent an injury to your pet.

CAGE ACCESSORIES

Although your iguana's habitat may become as elaborate as your imagination will allow, the bare minimum consists of: 1.) a cage, 2.) a substrate, 3.) lighting, 4.) a heater, 5.) food and water bowls, and 6.) a climbing apparatus. The last two entries are basically self-explanatory but deserve some discussion. Nearly any tree branch will suffice for climbing, but cleanliness must be kept in mind. If you're bringing in twigs or driftwood from outdoors make sure that they are clean, mite-free and dry. Open wood can harbor germs, parasites and bacteria so, as a precaution, soak it in a mild bleach solution, followed by a thorough rinse and drying. This technique is borrowed from the tropical fish hobbyist who will bleach and rinse driftwood, coral, etc., to prevent the contamination of aquarium water. If you find that you have an iguana that is infested with mites, you

simple incandescent fixture placed in or above the top of the cage will suffice, with a 50- to 75-watt bulb supplying the radiant heat. Remember that the iguana will attempt to get as close as possible to the source of heat and that serious burns could

should use this process as a follow-up to treat the animal and prevent reinfestation from mites and their nits (eggs) hidden in the wood.

For the food and water containers, use sturdy bowls that will not be tipped over easily. My favorite are the large stone crocks used for dog dishes. A rock in the water dish will help anchor it and provides an island for water-seeking crickets which would otherwise drown.

There are many ways to provide an iguana with its required heat. One is through the use of under-tank heating pads. Such pads are economical and efficient, and give an animal a choice between heated and unheated zones. Most pet stores carry under-tank heating pads. Photo courtesy of Hagen.

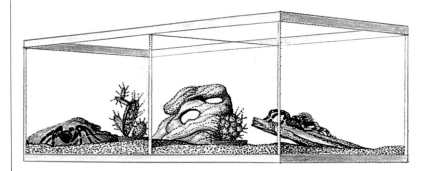

A low, long, desert cage is perhaps the worst possible habitat for a healthy, growing iguana. Learn about your lizard's needs before you buy one.

Many large iguanid lizards are both arboreal (living in trees) and herbivorous (eating only or mostly vegetables). A colony of spiny-tailed iguanas, *Ctenosaura*, is occupying this large tree in Costa Rica.

CAGE MAINTENANCE

Plan on changing the iguana's food and water supply on a daily basis. There may be exceptions when the water appears untouched, but since many iguanas use their water supply for a toilet, you should usually change it as a precaution. I like to use a drop of an aquarium water dechlorinating solution in the water to help neutralize chlorine and chloramine, common additives to city water supplies. The avoidance of unwanted chemicals such as these may

Many amateur herpetologists would like to keep very large lizards, but they must be reminded that big lizards may create problems. The best coverage available of the group, which includes not only iguanas but monitors and tegus, is Robert Sprackland's *Giant Lizards* (T.F.H. Publications).

seem like a trivial detail, but it is a very worthwhile precaution, as is the avoidance of chemically preserved fruits and vegetables for your pet's food. These chemicals are designed to be safe for human consumption, but can have detrimental effects on an animal which is a small fraction of a human's body weight and lacks the elaborate kidney-liver filtering mechanisms of a human. You can feed your pet every day or every other day, but remove the food bowl after about eight hours or overnight. The uneaten food will spoil causing unwanted smells and bacteria. Depending on the size of your lizard and the number you keep, a thorough cage cleaning should take place on the average of once a week. Stray food, dead crickets and feces should be removed as soon as they are noticed, but the whole tank should get a once-over on a weekly basis.

THE IGUANA AS A COMMUNITY LIZARD

By observing several iguanas in a cage together, piled on top of a heat rock or stacked three-deep on a branch, one would get the impression that these lizards

GIANT LIZARDS

ROBERT GEORGE SPRACKLAND

are gregarious and would be lost without each other's

company. Although iguanas are found in multiples in the wild and are often caged together dozens at a time, there are some indications contrary to the assumption that these are society animals. Iguanas are territorial lizards and will defend their territories fiercely when intruded upon. Both the defender and the intruder may bob heads, extend their dewlaps, and bite savagely, sometimes resulting in deep lacerations or even broken limbs. A new iguana introduced to a tank with one or more established residents will often be

Facing page: Small lizards may be difficult to handle. This *Anolis sagrei* could easily run up the girl's arm and escape, only to die from exposure to unsuitable weather. Iguanas are just as easy to lose as anoles, so be careful.

antagonized for a while, but may be accepted after a period of "initiation" and treated with the usual indifference iguanas show to each other. In the wild, iguanas will fight when the boundaries of their territory are crossed—the males during breeding season are said to be the most quarrelsome. Case in point: iguanas are usually tolerant of each other but never dependent upon each other. Most new pet owners ask if a solitary iguana will be lonely; the answer is, of course not. A single iguana will do as well, if not better, than one kept in a colony, and since males and females are similar in appearance and temperament, there is no need to be concerned with buying one or the other. I personally have a couple of reasons for buying iguanas in groups of two, rather obscure reasons I'll admit, but worth considering nonetheless. First, if you ever desire to have more than one iguana, it is easier to raise two initially than to introduce a new one later. Your first iguana would likely defend its cage adamantly. Second, in the event that one of the lizards becomes sick or dies in later years, most pet owners will feel a lesser emotional loss if

there is a survivor. Third, any deviation in the health of one animal will be noticed more quickly if contrasted to the other healthier more active one (assuming, of course, that both animals do not become ill at the same time). I have had many iguanas brought to me when they are beyond hope by pet owners who simply do not notice any symptoms of an illness until it is too late ("I thought it was hibernating!"). A good number of these pets could have been saved if an aberrancy in their behavior had been detected sooner, and I feel that having another iguana to compare with would have helped.

Aside from being compatible with other lizards, our pet is usually passive toward other species of lizard, making it a good community animal. The community cage is becoming more popular with reptile owners and keeping several species of lizard together in a large environment presents an attractive, educational situation. There are many lizards which are eligible cagemates, but only consider ones with similar dispositions: basilisks, curly-tails, swifts and water dragons are good choices. Avoid the larger and more

aggressive monitors, tegus, tokay geckos and the like; most are unpredictable and very carnivorous. Avoid also the smaller and more bite-size types such as anoles, ground skinks, etc., as they can easily be mistaken and taken for food by a cricket-eater. Most other lizards will enjoy the same heat and light requirements of the Green Iguana; the biggest difference will be the need for a continuous supply of insects, since most other lizards will not share the iguana's diet.

WHERE TO BUY YOUR PET

Deciding where to buy your iguana is a big step and deserves much consideration. In a given city or area, you may find several stores that carry these reptiles, and unless you are already a "regular" at a reliable pet shop, you may have to visit a few before making your choice. Phone shopping may narrow down the possibilities, but in most cases you will have to visit the stores in person. Most cities have reptile clubs; try

Buy your iguana from a pet shop that takes good care of all its animals. Stress is one of the major causes of death in captive lizards. These spiny swifts, *Sceloporus jarrovi*, seem healthy and active.

calling one and asking for the recommendation of the most reliable pet shop in the area. Contacting the instructor of herpetology at your local high school or university is also a good idea.

Try to find a good pet shop in which reptiles are a specialty, not a sideline. When visiting a pet shop, try to get a good general feel for how the animals are cared for. Before you look at the lizards themselves, look at their cages. Cleanliness here is essential. If the cage is littered with old food, droppings, etc., it may be time to consider another outlet. Another obvious sign of neglect is the condition of the animals' water and food dishes. An iguana's water bowl should be filled with fresh clean water daily; old stagnant water or a dried-up bowl would indicate improper care. If the food bowl is full, check for the proper diet. If the food bowl is empty, it is not necessarily a bad sign (they're eating), but if the food is old or moldy, make note of it. The next thing you'll want to check is if the iguana's light and heat requirements are being met. If the room in which the reptiles are being kept seems uncomfortably warm, consider that a plus in favor of your future pet's health. There is probably no better insurance against sick iguanas than keeping them at a consistent high temperature. If the tank itself is not exceedingly warm, try checking the temperature of the cage by placing your hand against it. It should be heated internally by a heating pad, heat rock, or similar device, and therefore feel warmer than room temperature. If the store's reptile facilities fail both of these tests, consider the possibility that an iguana purchased here may later suffer from respiratory maladies, digestive problems or other ailments due to its being kept at too low a temperature even though it may appear healthy at present. Although nearly any type of light fixture may be used to illuminate the cage, an iguana, which is destined to spend its life indoors, needs a source of artificial sunlight. In checking the pet shop's light fixtures, you should find them loaded with fluorescent bulbs of an appropriate variety. These bulbs are originally designed for greenhouse applications and are made to synthesize the sun's natural wave lengths, allowing the pet to use the vitamins and enzymes within its system,

**SPECIALIZING IN
RARE AND EXOTIC REPTILES
FINEST QUALITY • LARGEST SELECTION**

much the way it would in the wild. Fortunately, the deficiencies brought about by a lack of sunlight usually take some time to manifest themselves, and a baby iguana taken from this improper environment and placed in one with correct lighting should show no lasting signs of ill health.

Once this mental checklist has been completed, you should have formed a strong negative or positive opinion of the store in which you are shopping. This is no guarantee, of course, that the iguanas you are about to consider will be good or bad as a result of it, merely a guideline as to the care they are receiving. Put this first impression aside for the time being; it's time to look at the lizards themselves.

If there are more than one or two iguanas from which to choose, that's good; if there are several, that's better still and you may already notice some of the

Iguanas often remind people of dinosaurs and the Cretaceous, but of course they are not related to the dinosaurs any more than are turtles or snakes. This fascinating poster depicts an island iguana, *Cyclura*, as its centerpiece.

As you become more interested in reptiles and amphibians, you will want larger books to help answer your questions. One of the best is *The Completely Illustrated Atlas of Reptiles and Amphibians* from T.F.H. Publications, which covers almost every type of herp known.

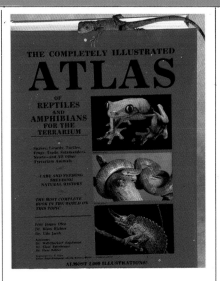

examples looking better or worse than others. While coloration may play a role in your final decision, bear in mind that iguanas that start their lives with bright green and blue tones to their skin often fade to lighter greens and browns in later years. Iguanas also possess some chameleonic abilities and can alter their color somewhat due to physiological and psychological factors; incidentally, it is not unheard of to find newly imported iguanas whose colors have been enhanced artificially.

Take into consideration that a young iguana under the right conditions should be in a state of constant growth, and that at any given time one or more areas of its body may be shedding its old outgrown skin. This is a healthy sign and, although it may give a somewhat tattered look to the animal, it is a good indication of appetite and general well-being. However, if an iguana's skin is loose-fitting and uniform green color with no signs of shedding or peeling anywhere, he's been wearing the same suit too long—you should find a lizard with a better appetite. An iguana that's been eating should have a nicely rounded stomach with no loose folds of skins along its sides. Its tail should be plump where it meets the body, not frail and bony-looking. Like most other reptiles, iguanas can go considerable lengths of time without eating. To survive this, the animal must ingest its own fat supplies, the biggest storage areas of this being in the back legs and tail. An iguana that appears thin in these areas has probably been deprived of food for quite a while, refusing to eat, or is infested with parasites that are robbing it of the nourishment it normally receives from eating.

As far as what kind of behavior to expect from the iguanas that you are observing, generally the

This pair of Green Anoles *(Anolis carolinensis)* is preparing to mate. Male lizards commonly grab the females by the nape of the neck to help move them into mating position.

Uma notata, a sand-dwelling iguanid from the western American deserts.

healthiest examples will be the wilder more active ones. Reaching into a tank of baby iguanas should send them skittering in all directions, not at all anxious to be picked up or handled. While iguanas are noted among the reptile group as being an easily tamable species, this is not to suggest that they are slow, calm or even docile by nature. This misconception often leads a customer to choose a slow, passive iguana over a more skittish one, because it would appear to make a better pet. What they are actually choosing is a sickly animal, one too complacent to show any aggression or resist being handled. Put the health of the animal first, the potential to be a tame pet second. If an iguana runs to avoid human handling, fine. It is only showing the proper instincts of a wild animal, which it is. If it bites, scratches, thrashes its tail or shows any other signs of aggression, better still—this spunky attitude and will to survive are the positive attributes of a healthy iguana. There will be plenty of time to tame your pet later; for now, be content to select one that is likely to live a long time.

General Maintenance and Care

DIET

When an iguana hatches from its egg, it will be, like most other lizards, an insectivore. When hungry, it will forage for beetles, grubs, crickets and probably anything else that wiggles enough to catch its wary eye. Although a few iguanas will continue these carnivorous feeding habits throughout their adult lives, including small mice and other rodents in their fare, most enjoy a gradual shift of diet to

Many iguanas are herbivorous, which means a keeper doesn't have to bother with such tedious chores as buying and maintaining cricket or mouse colonies. Convenient "food cubes" are now commercially available for such iguanas, thoughtfully formulated to provide all the essential nutrients required for peak health. Photo courtesy of Ocean Nutrition.

Facing page: If you start training them early, some iguanas can be trained to take food from the hand.

include more vegetable matter. After the first few months to a year, the average iguana will be mainly vegetarian or at least omnivorous, although it is doubtful that a hungry iguana in the wild will ever turn up its nose at a young mouse! An iguana will form feeding habits in the wild, dependent on the availability of different foods in its particular area, and, as it becomes more arboreal, the various leaves, flowers, berries and bananas it finds in treetop excursions will become the staple of its diet.

As iguana "parents," we must try to duplicate the foods that a captive iguana had already been eating in the wild as well as supply the options it will soon encounter as its diet pattern changes, all the while steering it toward a well-balanced diet. Hopefully this controlled diet will be at least as nourishing, if not more so, than the one it would have survived on in the wild. A wild iguana's diet is left entirely up to chance. When buying a new iguana, it will be necessary to pinpoint what foods it already accepts before introducing new foods to balance the diet. If the pet shop from which you purchased the iguana cannot tell you what it has been eating (it should), you must play a guessing game for a while in order to find out. A new iguana may require several days of acclimation to recover its normal

A diet heavy in lettuce is not sufficiently nutritious to maintain a healthy iguana. Be sure to provide a varied diet.

appetite so don't be alarmed if the pet does not eat after a recent moving, although food should be offered anyway. A young iguana should be given live insects, crickets and mealworms—all of which should be readily procurable from most pet shops.

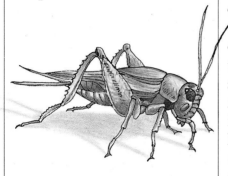

In addition to this, a bowl of food should be offered containing fresh fruits and vegetables and possibly a good canned cat or dog food. Examples from the vegetable group include spinach, broccoli, asparagus, cabbage and carrots, finely chopped or shredded. Raw or cooked squashes and pumpkins are good also. Favorite fruits include bananas, papayas, pineapples, kiwis and apples. Commercial baby foods containing these fruits in strained form are a good food source. Lettuce, while readily accepted by most iguanas, supplies very little nourishment and can therefore be dismissed in favor of dark green leafy

vegetables. Flowers are a common food in the wild and dandelions (with greens) are fine for the captive iguana and economical for you. If an iguana doesn't eat while you're watching, and many won't, it will be necessary to offer a variety of foods and survey the bowl on the following day to see what is missing. I like to organize the food bowl into thirds—vegetables on one side, then fruits, then dog food—to make the inspection easier. Remember, however, that if you're offering vegetable and insect matter simultaneously, a slight diminishing of the food supply overnight may mean only that your crickets are well fed.

With a new specimen, I

Young iguanas will take more animal protein than adults, and many learn to like crickets. Crickets can be purchased at your pet shop or raised at home at low cost. They are also easily dusted with vitamin and mineral supplements.

Young iguanas should be given supplements to ensure they receive all the vitamins and minerals they need to stay healthy and grow satisfactorily. Supplements may be liquids that can be licked from an eye dropper or powders put on the food.

will usually forgo the treatment of their food with vitamins and bone meal until the eating habits are firmly established, lest the taste of these additives discourage the animal from eating at all. If the iguana is extremely deficient or emaciated, I will supply vitamins orally with an eye dropper or by injection, in hopes that an association between bad tastes and food will not be made. Once feeding patterns are established, dusting the food with a vitamin supplement and bone meal should be done religiously. If the iguana is still eating live food, the same results can be achieved by shaking the insects in a bag with powdered vitamins and bone meal before placing them in the cage. Furthermore, if you plan to

indicate a potassium imbalance (bananas may help); diarrhea and weight loss can be combated by reducing or halting lettuce

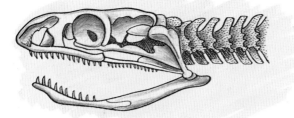

Snakes and lizards are closely allied, though snakes have much more flexible lower jaws than most lizards. An iguana skull would be more heavily plated than this snake skull.

keep or breed crickets or mealworms in a separate facility, their food supply (vegetables, cereal, etc.) can also be treated with vitamins to provide your iguana with fortified crickets. The health of your pet will rely largely on its diet and the bigger variety, the better. Since no one source of food will supply an iguana with all the nutrients it needs, try to encourage a broad array from the different food groups. If you find that you have a finicky eater, supply enough of its favorite foods to sustain it, add the vitamins, then mix in similar foods in an effort to enhance the diet. Simple correlations between the different food groups and a particular health problem taken from your own diet can help; for example, an eye problem could indicate a deficiency of carotene (carrots may help); a nervous condition could

intake; etc. While stories abound telling of twenty-year-old iguanas raised on diets consisting solely of pizza or cornflakes, they are to be considered the exception and not the norm and filed away with stories about "My uncle who lived to be ninety-seven and smoked five packs a day"—amusing anecdotes but poor health guidelines.

AN OUNCE OF PREVENTION

So you've had your iguana a few months or more without any significant problems. It's been eating well, growing at a steady rate and has needed far less care than you anticipated. One day, however, you notice that your normally active pet has been rather lackluster, rarely moving about the cage or visiting the food bowl. On closer

Facing page: Never stint on your pet's diet. Don't get into the habit of just throwing it a few pieces of lettuce in the morning before you leave for school or work. Iguanas are living animals and deserve your complete attention in order to keep them healthy. If you don't have the time to take care of your iguana properly, then consider getting some other type of pet.

inspection, it may appear limp, possibly pale in color and generally lethargic. Its bone structure may seem peculiarly ill-defined, especially at the back legs, which may appear puffy or swollen. The lower jaw will lack definition also, often to the point of feeling mushy and devoid of any bone support. The animal's wrists will feel as if the bones have dissolved, and they will be unable to support the iguana when it tries to walk. You are witnessing the effects of fibrous osteodystrophy, a leading killer of captive iguanas. How, you will ask, did your pampered pet acquire this disease? Does this life-threatening affliction of such diverse symptoms sneak up on your iguana overnight? Well, probably not. While, during the first week after its purchase, your pet was fed carefully prepared meals containing a wide variety of items recommended by your pet store, lately it has been much easier to throw in some lettuce each morning on the way to work. After all, it was doing so well that a little change in diet couldn't hurt, could it? Next you ran out of the special reptile vitamins you were talked into buying, but he acted the same without them, so you forgot

to buy more. Come to think of it, you never even bought the fluorescent light with the Vita-Lite bulb for its cage because it seemed too expensive. You've now diagnosed not only the iguana's disease but a very contagious pet-owner's disease as well—neglect. As humans, we tend to forget the importance of preventative medicine until a state of emergency arises. We forget to floss our teeth until they need fillings, forget to take our vitamins until we are sick, forget to exercise until we are obese, and unfortunately, adopt these same principles in our pet care. Since the iguana showed no outward signs of distress, had food and water and seemed fat enough (i.e., the puffy back legs), we saw fit to forgo all precautionary care and let its health deteriorate until it was too late. Since iguanas don't tell us much about how they feel, make sure that you monitor their health closely and take note of even the most subtle changes. The effect of fibrous osteodystrophy, by the way, can be arrested if caught in its early stages, although the accompanying bone damage cannot be reversed. By concentrated injections of vitamin D_3 and calcium

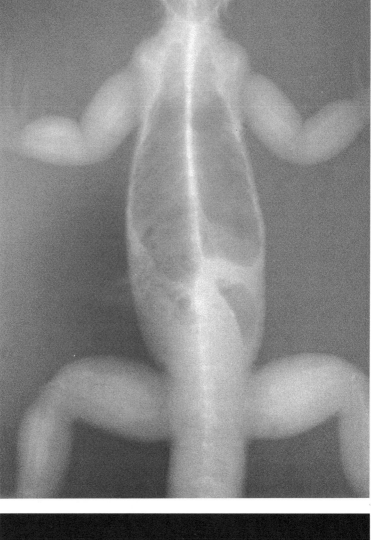

Metabolic bone disease (osteodystrophy) is a killer of many iguanas in captivity. The legs become swollen and the tissues dense so that in X-rays the bones are barely visible (top, as compared to normal animal on facing page). The muscle tissue is severely atrophied (bottom). From Dr. Fredric Frye's *Reptile Care*.

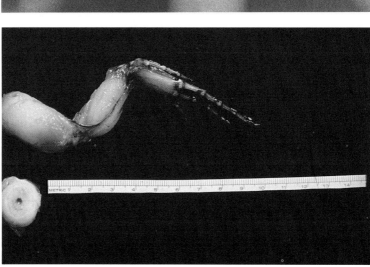

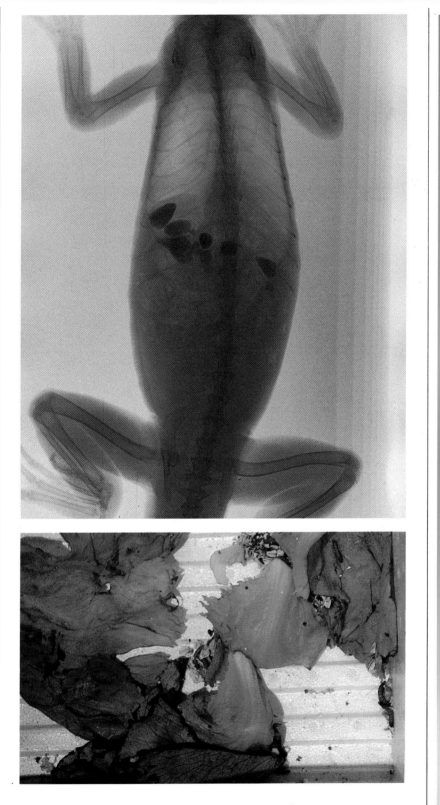

X-ray of a normal iguana showing well-developed bones. At the bottom is the remains of a meal sure to cause poor bone growth and eventual death: lettuce, mealworms, and rolled oats. From Dr. Fredric Frye's *Reptile Care*.

gluconate, long periods of exposure with a sun lamp, and immediate correction of the diet along with the addition of vitamins and bone meal to the food may keep the illness in check. The author cannot over-emphasize the value of preventative measures to keep your iguana in tiptop shape and free of illnesses.

PARASITES

There are other health problems that may trouble the iguana that are much less the fault of the pet owner—one of these is infestation of parasites. It would be safe to say that every iguana newly imported from its native habitat, much less every one which has come in contact with other imported lizards in the pet shop, has been exposed to some sort of parasite. The most common parasites are external—mites and ticks. The easiest way to deal with them is to assume that your new pet has them and use prophylactic treatment when you first bring it home. Much like treating a dog with fleas, treating an iguana for mites is a two-fold process as both the animal and the cage must be attended. By treating the pet when you first bring it home, you eliminate the possibility of re-infestation

from the cage or surroundings. With tweezers in hand, give your iguana a once-over in search of ticks first. They will appear as fairly large (2–5 mm.) brown disc-like objects protruding from the skin, usually around the front quarters and dewlap. They are usually quite firmly embedded and will require a

A healthy Water Dragon in a roomy cage with many climbing branches, basking areas, and water in which to swim.

good tug to get them out. Treat the spot from which you removed the tick with a light antiseptic as it may bleed, and drop the ticks into alcohol or peroxide to render them lifeless before they find a new host, such as the family dog. While tick-hunting, search your iguana for mites also. You are unlikely to see them (they're tiny), although on a badly infested animal you may be able to see them scurrying about on the iguana's head. You are more likely to see the droppings of the mites, a fine white dust or specks in the infested areas. Regardless of whether or not you see evidence of mites, it is wise to treat the iguana as a precaution.

A Water Dragon with a severely abraded snout caused by continually rubbing on its cage in an attempt to escape. Such raw snouts are typical of stressed animals and may lead to serious bacterial and fungal infections. From Dr. Fredric Frye's *Reptile Care*.

Fill a bathtub or sink with warm water and submerge the body of the iguana for several minutes in an effort to drown the mites. Be sure to keep the animal's nostrils above the water. This is admittedly easier said than done, since a full-grown

I suggest putting a new iguana in a simple quarantine cage for the first two weeks to keep any parasite problem in check. By no means should the new arrival be introduced to a community situation with other lizards, lest a parasite

iguana will not tolerate such treatment for too long. This is a good time also to wipe off any other foreign matter from the iguana's skin, such as droppings from other iguanas, and to peel off shedding skin. Other recommended remedies* call for the application of 90-percent grain alcohol and castor oil (in equal proportions) and the dusting of your pet with Dri Die 67, a dehydrating agent, or Sulphanone, a mite poison that is safe to use on iguanas.

*CAUTION: Dri Die and many other mite treatments may kill a small iguana already weakened by diseases and heavy infestations. Extreme care is advised.

problem or other communicable disorder spread. Somewhere in the quarantine cage (and future cages as well) hide a half-inch segment of an insecticide-impregnated plastic strip; I suggest a spot near the screen top where the iguana cannot lick or try to eat it. Never use any spray pesticides, roach killers or the like in or about the lizard's cage; remember that young iguanas are insectivores and may feed upon the poisoned bugs.

Views of an iguana suffering from severe metabolic bone disease brought about by a poor diet. The jaws and legs are swollen and bowed, and the fingers often are swollen and twisted. This disorder may be fatal in captive iguanas. From Dr. Fredric Frye's *Reptile Care*.

Notice the greatly swollen jaws and legs of this iguana, signs of serious and perhaps terminal metabolic bone disease. From Dr. Fredric Frye's *Reptile Care*.

Internal parasites present a more difficult problem for the pet owner. A variety of parasitic worms plague the lizard families and the easiest way to eschew these parasites is to not choose a skinny, lackluster lizard from the onset. If, however, you suspect that your iguana is suffering from internal parasites, contact your veterinarian or pet shop immediately. Although several over-the-counter cat and dog wormers are reported to be successful in treating this problem, gauging the right dosage for the weight of your animal is tricky and a lethal dosage could be administered accidentally.

RESPIRATORY PROBLEMS

Iguanas, like most other reptiles, are prone to colds and respiratory problems. The cause is usually a cold draft or an exceedingly low ambient temperature. The cure, simple enough, is usually to increase the ambient temperature, often to around the 100–105°F range. This will speed up the animal's metabolism and help it fight off the illness on its own, although in some cases an antibiotic or vitamin injection may be in order—again consult your vet or trusted pet shop. These problems are easily avoided in the first place by keeping your iguana warm enough, so don't get lazy and ignore the heat.

MOUTH ROT

Infectious stomatitis, commonly called mouth rot, can plague many reptiles, and iguanas are no exception. It affects the gums and inner mouth area and may appear as an inflammation or as a yellowish cheesy patch in the animal's mouth. An early warning sign may be a lack of appetite (the affliction will cause discomfort in eating), a discharge around the mouth, or an ill-fitting jaw. Treatment involves swabbing the area with sulfamethiazine, panamycin, or commercial mouth rot remedies consisting of iodine mixed with a broad-spectrum antibiotic. As with many ailments, the chances of your buying an iguana

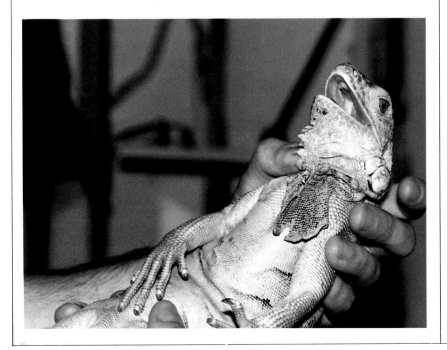

Check your iguana's mouth for signs of mouth rot, a bacterial disease more formally known as infectious stomatitis. This disease can kill your lizard, but it can be successfully treated.

with this illness are far greater than the iguana's being stricken with it later, so once again be cautioned about carefully picking out a healthy pet.

INJURIES

In the controlled environment you set up for your pet, there should be minimal chance of its hurting itself; nonetheless, accidents do happen. A common problem with newly imported iguanas is the raw abrasion of snout cage reduced to a simple quarantine set-up (i.e., a clean aquarium with paper toweling substrate). To prevent re-injury, provide the animal with a hiding place within the cage; chances are that it will seek refuge in this rather than persistently trying to tunnel out. Make the animal's health more important than having the animal on display, and let it adjust to captivity in its own due time.

Tail breakage is another common injury. While

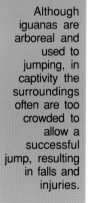

Although iguanas are arboreal and used to jumping, in captivity the surroundings often are too crowded to allow a successful jump, resulting in falls and injuries.

area caused by rubbing against the interior of the cage. A restless pet may scrape its head back and forth across the screen or glass in its endless attempts to escape, oblivious to the damage being done. As with any open wound the affected area should be treated with a local antiseptic/antibiotic, and the usually occurring during our own negligent handling, the tail can also become caught under a rock or branch in the cage and become detached when the animal tries to run away. Although the stump left by the missing tail may look quite grisly, it will begin to heal quickly and a replacement tail will start to regenerate in its place. A

Young iguanas are quite social if required to be social and adapt well to captivity. However, they do best if caged alone and handled as little as necessary to ensure they are docile.

lizard's ability to grow a second tail may be somewhat exaggerated however, and it may take months or even years for a suitable substitute to be completed. A replacement tail will not have the alternate green and black banding usually found on the original, but will instead be uniformly dark in coloration. Since the vertebrae, nerves and

consistently high during any convalescence and provide daily vitamin and bone meal supplements to the iguana's food; these additions will help the iguana in its task of rebuilding new tissues.

"I'M NOT HUNGRY"

An iguana's apathy to food can generally be linked to at least one of four causes: 1.) STRESS (psychological reasons), 2.) TEMPERATURE

No, no, no! Avoid the temptation to feed lettuce as a normal part of the diet. Lettuce is not actually harmful, it just contains almost no nutrients and is just too easy to sluff-off on an unsuspecting lizard.

muscles tissue will have been completely severed, the new tail will lack the complexity of movement associated with the old one and will be permanently devoid of true vertebrae. Treat the open wound with an antiseptic/antibiotic daily and use the quarantine-cage routine again as a precaution against secondary infections. Keep the temperature

(too high or low), 3.) DIET (improper food selection) and 4.) ILLNESS (bacterial, fungal, viral or parasitic conditions). Each of these we will cover categorically. In the first example, we review the problems encountered with a newly acquired specimen; in the second situation, we examine a disruption in the feeding schedule of a well-

Absolute minimal caging for a young iguana. Where are the climbing branches? Notice the dirty water in the swimming bowl (actually a small cat litter box). Unless cage conditions are improved soon, this little iguana may never get a chance to grow up.

acclimated iguana.

A New Specimen Refuses Food

STRESS: Minimize handling. Site cage remote from disturbances by people and other pets. Provide hide-box. Provide perch (iguanas feel more secure in an arboreal habitat). Isolate from other specimens.

TEMPERATURE: Raise temperature in the high-90s F. Provide a "realistic" light cycle (at least six to eight hours of darkness).

DIET: Experiment with a wider variety of foods. Experiment with different feeding times. Attempt to learn feeding habits from previous owner or pet shop. Forgo food additives (vitamins, etc.).

ILLNESS: Check for mouth rot, abrasions, sagging or ill-fitting jaw (symptoms of calcium deficiency/fibrous osteodystrophy) or any other abnormality which may cause discomfort in chewing. Check for mites and other parasites. Examine cage for feces. If the animal is not passing previously digested food, it will have little need to ingest more. A warm bath might stimulate the iguana to defecate, as may a few drops of mineral or cod liver oil administered orally with an eye dropper. Constipation should not last more than a few days before receiving professional attention, however. A very serious condition known as prolapsed rectum can occur

Serious injury can result from faulty hot rocks and unguarded lighting fixtures. The scar on this iguana's tail was caused by a burn it received as a hatchling.

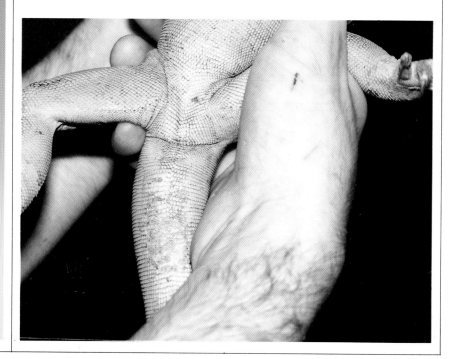

Holbrookia texana, a fast-running iguanid lizard of the North American deserts than can burrow into the loose sand in seconds, literally disappearing before your eyes.

when an iguana's bowels become obstructed and remain so for any considerable length of time. In the attempt to pass the blockage, such an animal's intestine becomes strained and will actually distend out of the cloaca. Do not delay in seeing a veterinarian if you detect symptoms of this condition.

A Well-Acclimated Iguana Refuses to Eat

STRESS: Provide hide-box and minimize handling. If you have recently added any new cagemates, remove them.

TEMPERATURE: Raise temperature to mid-90s°F. In rare cases of extreme high temperatures, aestivation may occur; in this case, reduce temperatures to 75–85°F by providing shade, misting with water, adding a large basin of cool water to the cage, etc.

DIET: Tempted with a wider variety of foods, your pet may overcome its boredom with its usual fare. For cricket-eaters, try alternative live foods such as earthworms, pinkie mice, caterpillars or minnows. For vegetable eaters, try these live options also, in addition to more fresh fruits, edible flowers and cooked squash or pumpkin.

ILLNESS: Check for parasites, mouth rot, constipation and any other disorder which may interrupt normal eating habits. Occasionally a build-up of unshed skin will constrict an iguana and cause discomfort. If you suspect this condition (skin is dry, taut, pale in color), try frequent baths and rubbing mineral oil into the skin. Shedding should take place soon and the animal's appetite should resume. Taking a few minutes to give the animal a good once-over from time to time is a good idea, regardless of its outward appearance. In this way, many ailments can be detected in their early stages instead of waiting until they have advanced to a life-threatening condition. The physical examination may reveal broken toes or claws, sometimes even limbs; cuts and abrasions from quarrels with cagemates or sharp obstructions within the cage; blisters from overzealous heat rocks, etc.

FORCE-FEEDING

There are times when an iguana will try our patience with its abstinence from food. It is out of this frustration that we, as pet owners, often turn to offering commercial appetite stimulants, administering vitamin injections, and cramming food objects down the throats of our reluctant pets. It is the intention of this author, rather than offer a "how to" lesson on force-feeding, to explain how, when and why *not* to force-feed your pet. The point of logic behind this is that force-feeding usually takes place to satisfy the needs of the pet owner, not the pet itself. I have received far too many calls with the opening remark, "My iguana didn't eat for five days so I force-fed it, what should I do?" The pet owner, disappointed by the unwillingness of his iguana to attack its food, decided to take nature into his own hands and force food into the animal with no

regard to one basic and important factor—maybe it wasn't hungry. Sure it's frustrating when an iguana goes days or weeks without eating, but in most cases the combination of temperature, diet alternatives, a hide-box, and most of all, patience, will yield the desired results. If you lack the compassion to let your iguana eat on its own terms, perhaps an aquarium full of piranha would be a better choice.

The second point in the anti-force-feeding argument is simple: if the leading cause of anorexia in reptiles is stress (from a recent move, an aggressive cagemate, incorrect temperatures, etc.), why do we seek to remedy this problem by restraining the animal, prying its mouth open, and stuffing food down its throat? It seems obvious that by creating this additional stressful situation for the iguana, we can only prolong the problem and postpone the resumption of its natural feeding habits. It is also incorrect for us to assume that as long as nourishment is entering the iguana—regardless of how artificial the means— somehow things are "all right," and the animal is healthy. Nothing could be further from the truth, although you could probably

sustain the animal for quite some time in this manner instead of correcting the original problem. While a reluctance to eat may occur under perfectly healthy conditions—a reptile's prerogative, if you will—it may be the sign of a much more serious problem. If the iguana is trying to tell us something by its fasting, it is our duty to observe the signals, interpret the data, and remedy the illness—not mask the symptoms by force-feeding. This theory also applies to the so-called appetite stimulants available commercially. Even if the chemical concoction could, over a period of time, induce the animal to eat, the additional stress the iguana experiences by forcing ingestion of these oral medications seems counter-productive at best.

There will be times, of course, when force-feeding will prevail as the only alternative to losing the specimen. At this time, you will have to use strict criteria to decide if the iguana should be given this artificial life-support method or not, and if so, how to administer it. For instance, is a period of force-feeding necessary to get an iguana over the hump of an illness or condition (severe stomatitis, broken

jaw, etc.) which is preventing the animal from eating naturally, or is it likely that this method will be needed to sustain the specimen throughout the remainder of its life? Is the iguana suffering a period of convalescence in which it would be better off relying on the ingestion of its own fat deposits than risking the strain of trying to digest nourishment given orally? I have witnessed specimens with a severe illness (e.g., advanced fibrous osteodystrophy) sustain themselves for weeks on their own resources, sometimes to a full recovery and sometimes, of course, to death, while a similar specimen in a parallel situation expired quickly after the force-feeding intended to save it. This can only imply that the strain of trying to digest the food forced into its system was too exhausting for an animal in such a weakened state, especially bearing in mind that force-feeding often results in regurgitation.

General rules of thumb: 1.) Force-feed only as a last resort. 2.) Use only a puree or soft, easily digestible mixture when force-feeding. 3.) Never force-feed an animal live insects. A live cricket or mealworm, for instance, which would normally be bitten or chewed before swallowing, could easily bore a hole through the iguana's stomach if swallowed whole and unharmed. Try tricking the iguana into eating before resorting to force-feeding. Usually some baby food or apple sauce will be lapped off willingly if the iguana's nose is rubbed in it, as will most liquids allowed to drip on the animal's nose from an eye dropper.

EUTHANASIA

Although it is an unpleasant alternative to consider for our pet, sometimes a decision must be made whether or not a sick iguana should be sustained or put to sleep. Situations arise in which the finest veterinary attempts will not arrest an illness; in other cases, such as a severe calcium deficiency, the ailment itself may be treated successfully, but the accompanying bone damage will linger on, causing permanent discomfort. It is impossible to judge in human terms how much pain a sick or injured iguana may be enduring, but it is safe to say that in some cases we would be doing the humane thing by ending the animal's suffering. A

Corytophanes hernandezi of Central America is one of several iguana-like lizards that sometimes appear on the pet market. This Helmeted Iguana is rather delicate.

reptile's sensitivity to pain is directly proportionate to its body temperature so, to alleviate the iguana's suffering and consequently cause its demise, we must slowly cool the animal down until it expires. A pan of cool water (50–60°F) will initiate the anesthesia; gradually diminishing the temperature of the water (35–40°F) will cause the iguana to become torpid, and placing the container of water in the freezer will gradually cool the iguana to the point where all bodily functions cease. We hope that you will never have to resort to such measures, but knowing this expedient and humane procedure can help you deal with the unpleasant task of euthanasia in a graceful manner.

The Tale of The Popeye

This is a story of a grossly mistreated pet. At its worst it may suggest that the sale of exotic animals should somehow be restricted to those who have prior knowledge or experience and the responsibility which accompanies such a purchase. At best it shows that an animal, through some stroke of luck, can survive even the most blatant human neglect.

"Popeye" arrived at my residence a little after midnight on a Thursday evening. Resting in the bottom of a paper sack in 30°· Michigan weather, it would be hard to imagine more adverse conditions to the survival of a sick South American reptile. Popeye had been returned that night to the pet shop from which it was purchased by a dissatisfied customer, doubtlessly blaming either the store or the iguana itself for its poor state of health. A friend of mine, who happened to be shopping there, witnessed the transaction and convinced the store's management to give him the chronically ill iguana in lieu of disposing of it, promising to deliver it to someone who may have a chance of helping it. Upon receiving the animal, I set up a heated isolated tank (simply as a matter of course, recognizing full well the chance that it might be carrying a communicable illness or parasite which could be transferred to my healthy specimens) and began assessing its condition.

It had classic symptoms of fibrous osteodystrophy. It was very emaciated although the "honeycombing" caused by the disease had swollen its limbs and joints to such an extent that it appeared muscle-bound. It was from this characteristic and the jowl-like appearance of its lower jaw that the name was suggested, and, although I didn't expect to see the iguana live more than a few days, we christened the new arrival "Popeye." I prepared a shot of calcium gluconate to administer subcutaneously in one of the animal's rear legs, exercising caution that the puffy framework, which was once a healthy femur, was not shattered by the injection. I secured a fluorescent fixture above the open top of the aquarium (I didn't foresee its leaping out) with the proper broad-spectrum bulb and, since the iguana could barely drag itself around, replaced the usual water bowl with a shallow glass ashtray which could be "handicap-accessible." Although it was obviously stressed, I chose to forgo the usual addition of a hide-box for fear that it would restrict its exposure to the much needed sunlight. Instead I opted to cover the four sides of the tank with opaque cardboard, ensuring the movements about the room by myself or by my ever-inquisitive cats did not put the convalescing iguana on the defensive.

Confident that it was as comfortable as its condition would allow, I decided to retire, but as an afterthought

to skin and bones (and not much in the way of bones) by human error. I can sympathize with the new iguana owner who, despite doting over his pet and paying every attention to the animal's needs, must watch his pet waste away due to its refusal to eat. However, when an iguana is this receptive to food, even in a new environment, and in this state of ill health, I am at a loss to understand why its owner could not provide better care. I can only assume that when the novelty of owning a new pet wore off, its keeper regressed to feeding it such empty foods as tomatoes, lettuce, or possibly nothing at all.

offered a plate of food. Much to my dismay, it ate. Never had I seen a lizard in such a decrepit state show such interest in food, and, judging by its condition, I had naturally assumed that it had been refusing to eat for some time (hence its return to the pet shop) and therefore would have to be tube-fed for a week or so until its health improved or until euthanasia became inevitable. As much as its display of appetite excited me, it frustrated me as well to see the animal retain such a basic instinct to live, despite having been reduced

Popeye's first meal in its new residence consisted of waxworms (a soft caterpillar-ish grub) and broccoli. Since I keep my waxworms living in a vitamin and bone meal mixture, I intended these and injectable supplements to initiate the recovery process. Although it was willing to eat, the sunken deformity of its lower jaw caused its coordination to be sorely lacking. When in its first attempt it was unable to consume any food, I learned to pile its fare into a mound so that its awkward lunges actually resulted in some food staying in its mouth. In

O.K., so it's wearing a harness. But how do you get it out of the tree? Letting your iguana climb a tree outside may lead to loss of the iguana.

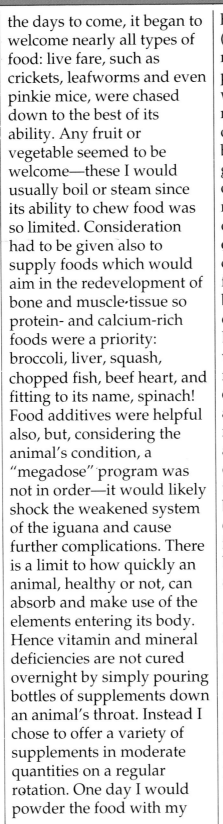

the days to come, it began to welcome nearly all types of food: live fare, such as crickets, leafworms and even pinkie mice, were chased down to the best of its ability. Any fruit or vegetable seemed to be welcome—these I would usually boil or steam since its ability to chew food was so limited. Consideration had to be given also to supply foods which would aim in the redevelopment of bone and muscle·tissue so protein- and calcium-rich foods were a priority: broccoli, liver, squash, chopped fish, beef heart, and fitting to its name, spinach! Food additives were helpful also, but, considering the animal's condition, a "megadose" program was not in order—it would likely shock the weakened system of the iguana and cause further complications. There is a limit to how quickly an animal, healthy or not, can absorb and make use of the elements entering its body. Hence vitamin and mineral deficiencies are not cured overnight by simply pouring bottles of supplements down an animal's throat. Instead I chose to offer a variety of supplements in moderate quantities on a regular rotation. One day I would powder the food with my handy reptile multi-vitamin (with a wide breakdown of minerals such as phosphorus, calcium, iron, as well as amino acids); the next day, bone meal, and so on with cod liver oil, brewer's yeast with garlic, ground egg shell, powdered oyster shell, etc. Luckily none of the food additives deterred its enthusiasm for eating, and, as it dutifully consumed small amounts of food once or twice daily, I began to sense that it may be on the road to recovery. Baths in shallow warm water were added to the daily regime both for reasons of exercise (limbering of atrophied joints) and rehydration. A sun lamp was applied for ten minutes daily, which, supplementing the full-spectrum fluorescent bulb burning twelve to eighteen hours a day, aided in carrying out the vitamin breakdown within the animal.

The task of caring for Popeye became more and more time-consuming. While a healthy iguana may subsist on a few minutes of concentrated daily care, along with a weekly cleaning and bath, one so degenerated as this becomes a full-time job. The maintenance routine on a sick reptile may stretch into hours each day, unfortunately with very few obvious results. Since days or weeks may pass before any noticeable improvements manifest themselves in the recuperating pet, we must be patient, as pet keepers, to continue the often frustrating task despite the lack of reward.

When caring for a large number of animals, you usually develop a certain emotional detachment from them. While not unsympathetic in regard to animals, acceptance of the fact that the odds of mortality will consume a few of the specimens is essential and bound to create a degree of callousness to these losses. I have always tried to maintain a level of objectivity when dealing with animals, but many times have fallen short of this goal. At times it is easy dealing with multiples, i.e., batches of newly imported iguanas, being resigned to the fact that a mortality rate of ten to thirty percent is likely, no matter how meticulous the care. In this fashion, all the specimens can be treated equally with the same adequate care, and saving or losing one is not taken as a personal loss or triumph. At other times, it is impossible to retain this

scientific detachment and I find myself totally absorbed in the survival of one individual. This was the case with Popeye, and, when a "project" becomes a "pet," I tend to react with the same personal involvement as I did with my first iguana at age nine. Perhaps I am trying to undo the injustice done to this example in the hands of its previous owner, perhaps too I am attempting to right my own wrongs and compensate for the mediocre care which I gave to so many captive reptiles in my youthful years.

Despite the odds, Popeye continued to improve. After a two-week period, it began moving with some agility, and although it had undoubtedly suffered irreversible bone damage, it appeared to move with no great discomfort. It took nearly a month for its color to improve, but the pallid yellow-green, which so often accompanies this deficiency, gradually gave way to healthy tones of green and blue. Although its appetite continued to be ravenous, it was not until the fifth or sixth week that it seemed to gain any weight. I became accustomed to the pitiful sight of it dragging around an overly full belly on wizened spindly legs,

Iguanas differ considerably in color and pattern from individual to individual. They also differ to some extent depending on their origin.

reminding me of the undernourished of our own species. Eventually though, it began to fill out and replenish fat and muscle tissues that had been long depleted. The rebuilding process continued over the next few months, slowly with no appreciable setbacks. I am happy to say that Popeye made a full recovery and continued to remain a member of my collection. Still visible were the sunken jawbones, swollen femurs and fused joints, permanent reminders of the faint creature that appeared on my doorstep on that very untropical evening.

Constructing a Cage

Previously we explained the benefits of housing your iguanas in a commercially built glass aquarium. Since they will eventually outgrown any moderately priced tank, for personal preference, you may want to consider the option of building your own enclosure. A well-planned cage can be the key to easy iguana care, solving such problems as heating, lighting, cleanliness and the housing of large specimens when proper attention is given to its design. Your iguana cage can be a thing of beauty; using fine woods and staining them to match the decor of the room can add the complimentary touch of a piece of exotic furniture to your home. The custom installation of a cage can make good use of nook, corner or even an unused closet in your house, where the placement of a large aquarium would be impractical. In favor of the animal's health, the larger enclosures made possible by the build-your-own concept can have a positive effect on your iguana's welfare as well. A large cage can more accurately recreate the freedom of movement that an iguana enjoys in the wild, while providing a variety of habitat situations (i.e., light and dark places, high perches versus low hide-boxes, etc.) from which the iguana can chose. Although supplying sufficient heat to a large cage requires a little more ingenuity than solving similar problems in a small glass aquarium, the wider range of temperatures available in the former allows the iguana to thermo-regulate its own body temperature more naturally. By heating only certain regions of the cage to a high temperature, while leaving others at room temperature or slightly above, the iguana can move freely about its environment seeking the optimum body temperature for its digestion and metabolism. Reptiles possess an amazing ability to collect, conserve and dissipate heat from external sources to keep their bodies at a stable temperature, often constant within one or two degrees Fahrenheit over a period of hours, despite wider fluctuations in the ambient temperature of their surroundings. Throughout our discussion, we have stressed the importance of high temperatures to the proper maintenance of tropical lizards such as the Green Iguana. While in fact it is true that low temperatures are hazardous, the healthiest environment for your iguana (or any reptile, for that matter) offers both high- and low-temperature areas. However, this dual-temperature environment set-up has a glitch.

While even the most competent pet shop clerk whom you may encounter may advise to provide a hot side and a cool side in any reptile's cage, the necessary advice he leaves out is to *avoid extremes.* Countless reptiles have been lost by not following this very important rule simply because the temperature choices offered, by reptilian standards, are just too vast. True, a reptile will seek out the warm spots of its habitat when instincts tell it that its body is cooling off. The problem occurs when the iguana (or python, tortoise, etc.) fails to vacate the source of heat when its body has had enough. The iguana's somewhat dull-witted nervous system coupled with a high tolerance for pain compound this problem, resulting in an animal which will not only seek out a source of heat but unfortunately stay at this locale until tissue damage results. If the heat source in your cage is a light bulb, space heater or poorly constructed heat rock, you are inviting trouble, especially if you think. an iguana is intelligent enough to move from a source of warmth when it is being scalded. I have seen iguanas lose toes, tails, entire limbs and sometimes become completely incinerated due to excessive heat. As a point of caution, test all heating units regularly. If you cannot keep the back of your bare hand on the heat rock, heating pad or the like for an extended period of time without discomfort, the

heating unit should be discarded or suitably housed so that the iguana cannot make direct contact with it. All lighting fixtures should be well out of the pet's reach also. Covering the bulb with a screen or grid should keep the iguana at a safe distance, although after long periods of exposure, a screen cover can get as warm as the bulb itself. Fluorescent bulbs heat much cooler than incandescents but have been known to burn specimens to a crisp nonetheless. The tips of these fixtures may get very hot (especially on older bulbs), so use the same precautions that you would apply to incandescents to be on the safe side.

Providing a cool area of the cage can be as misunderstood as providing adequate heat. By human standards, an ambient temperature of 50–60°F may seem slightly chilly but certainly not life-threatening. Our bodies continue to function more or less the same; our blood pumps at basically the same rate and our nervous system continues to perceive our surroundings with the same degree of accuracy. With ectothermal (or cold-blooded) animals, however, temperatures such as these become much more than just a minor inconvenience. The lower the temperature of the animal's surroundings, the lower its body temperature and bodily functions will be correspondingly slower. At the same room temperature that an endothermal (or warm-blooded) creature finds only mildly uncomfortable, an iguana's motor and nerve responses are starting to dull and its body is becoming sluggish. It is due to this phenomenon that many reptiles die thermal-related deaths in a cage that actually features an adequate heating system on one end of the habitat, but leaves the other end too cold. The chilled animal, while provided with a source of warmth well within reach, finds itself in a torpid and unresponsive state and is unable to adjust itself. For this reason, exercise caution when offering a choice of temperature situations for your iguanas. A variety is good, but keep it within reason in regard to a tropical ectothermal creature. Keeping the low end of the spectrum at 75–85°F is essential, so beware of building your cage in a basement, on a drafty floor, against large plate-glass windows, or by a door.

Increased ventilation is another advantage to a large custom-made cage. The stale uncirculated air of the small glass aquarium, with its higher levels of bacteria, nitrogen and carbon dioxide, can be an unhealthy atmosphere for your reptiles, although this too creates a paradox of sorts. A compromise must be struck between proper ventilation and efficient heat retention, since no one structure seems to inherently possess the best qualities of both. Although a glass aquarium can create a stuffy environment, there is no denying its ability to retain heat. Conversely, a large screen cage or wooden enclosure provides a fresh-airy atmosphere at the expense of being able to heat an isolated pocket of air. With this in mind, I suggest the use of multiple construction media for your custom cage. If the use of a screen is inevitable, restrict it to areas in the side or back of the cage, in turn using a more efficient insulator (i.e., plywood, formica, particle board) on the top of the cage to keep valuable heat from escaping. A nice alternative to a screen is the use of plexiglass perforated with occasional rows of drilled holes. It is pleasing visually and allows enough air to pass for good ventilation while restrictive enough to

Top: Shedding in an anole, *Anolis sagrei.* Iguanas usually shed in smaller patches than do anoles. *Bottom:* Mating Green Anoles. The male grasps the female and maneuvers her so their cloacas touch and his hemipene can be put in her cloaca.

conserve heat. If cost is a limiting factor, however, heavy screen or hardware cloth is generally the material of choice for use in areas where the cage must breathe.

An unpleasant by-product of a well-ventilated cage is the odors that originate from feces, moldy food and fouled water dishes, which start to invade the whole of the house. If you enjoyed the carefree maintenance schedule of keeping your young iguana in a small glass aquarium, it may not be that the tank never needed cleaning so much as the glass tank contained the smell to the point that you were not constantly reminded of it. Keeping your new cage free of troublesome "crooks and crannies," which may harbor bacteria, as well as proper selection of your flooring and substrate can help to minimize, if not eliminate, this aromatic problem. After some trial and error on my part, I found that the only substrate I can recommend positively for the large vivarium is indoor-outdoor carpeting.

Odors reach their peak when bacteria multiply on decomposing food and feces. The presence of moisture enhances this problem, so the natural ability of a

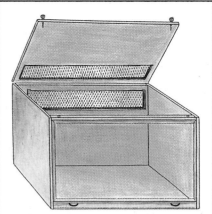

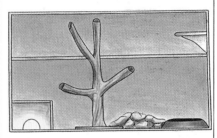

porous substrate to dissipate moisture and dehydrate the feces or food can be a big aid in controlling cage odors. Additional help can come from using a porous material under the artificial turf. An observation I have made while caring for an African Flap-neck Chameleon may help to illustrate.

The true chameleons of Africa and Europe are difficult at best to keep alive in captivity and many succumb within weeks despite the gallant efforts of pet keepers to meet their needs. Nonetheless, when I received a healthy example of a newly imported Flap-neck (*Chameleo dilepis*), I was determined to go to any

The cage must be ventilated or mildew and smells will build up inside. Mildewy cages are subject to more bacterial infections than sanitary cages.

extreme to ensure its survival and began customizing a large fish aquarium to suit its every whim. Since a finite set of rules is yet unestablished for successful chameleon care (and until such rules are, it is best to discourage the sale and keeping of this fascinating reptile), a lot of guesswork is involved. I wanted to employ all the near-absolutes that I knew to give this fragile lizard the benefit of the doubt. Unlike the iguana, and most other lizards as well, members of the chameleon family enjoy moderate, not high, temperatures (75–85°F being sufficient for most species). Chameleons also benefit from a high relative humidity, ironically a situation much easier to produce at iguana temperatures. Mimicking rain forest humidity in a glass aquarium is still fairly simple, usually accomplished by restricting the air containing evaporated water (from drinking containers, cage mistings, etc.) from exiting the top of the tank via replacement of the screen top with a glass or metal one. Easy enough were it not for the fact that chameleons also require an airy well-

ventilated cage, not a closed stuffy one. The humidity problem was solved by the installation of a water-drip system made from a small aquarium air pump which forced water up a plastic tube. The water would then flow from the top of the tube and splash down into a small fish bowl, humidifying the air and providing the ever-thirsty chameleon with the type of flowing water supply it prefers.

Baby iguanas have shorter snouts than adults, but they still tend to rub the snout on cage surfaces. Be sure any screened areas cannot be reached by the lizard, as screen may severely damage a snout.

Green Anoles often are called "American chameleons," but of course they really are related to the iguana and not to the true chameleons of Africa and adjacent areas.

Two other large iguanas. *Top:* An island iguana from the Caribbean, *Cyclura nubila.* *Bottom:* A basking colony of Galapagos Marine Iguanas, *Amblyrhynchus cristatus.* Both these species are protected by international laws and treaties.

Captive Breeding

A mere few years ago this chapter would possibly have been sub-titled "Don't Bother!" However, recent efforts by reptile enthusiasts coupled with decreased exportation of wild-caught specimens from tropical America indicate that successful captive-breeding programs may well be on the horizon. While scattered reports of captive iguana matings filter in, reasons for the failure of these matings to produce young are numerous, including but not

limited to: 1.) inadequate size of specimens, 2.) inadequate size of vivarium, 3.) improper diet and 4.) improper temperature and lighting.

First make sure that the specimens you choose to breed are of ample size and in excellent health. The mating process itself may be very rough, leaving one or both parties with injuries from claws and teeth. While the size of the male may not be crucial, the female must be large enough to bear the burden of carrying eggs without endangering her own health. A clutch of eggs ranging in number from twenty to seventy is possible;

with eggs averaging nearly one-and-a-half inches in diameter, it is easy to see the strain put on the female. I would recommend breeding females of no less than sixteen inches in body length (snout–vent length) to prevent jeopardizing the mother's health. Before laying, the gravid female may become so distended that it will become nearly impossible for it to move from place to place. At this time, it may also forgo eating—another reason to start with a sturdy healthy female iguana which will be able to survive on her fat supplies without risk to her own health or that of the

Top: A large iguana in the grass. Don't be misled that iguanas are slow-moving because they are cold-blooded. A warm iguana could easily outrun you over a short distance. *Bottom:* Mating Green Anoles. Notice that the male's tail is under the female's so their cloacas can touch.

clutch. The female's health can also be endangered by the natural re-direction of calcium within her system to the chore of egg-making. The manufacturing of thirty or so calcareous eggs may rob the parent of precious minerals, some egg-laying reptiles can actually starve from calcium deficiency during gestation. Once again, make sure that breeding specimens are in optimum shape to begin with and fortify their diet with ample vitamins and calcium supplements to prevent depletion.

Providing large enough quarters for your iguanas

Facing page: It may look cute to have your iguana roaming the house, but it is very dangerous. Few houses are warm enough or humid enough to suit an iguana for very long, and their heavy claws can badly damage furniture and clothing. In fact, the claws of even a tame adult iguana can cause serious scratches to exposed human skin—a word to the wise should be sufficient.

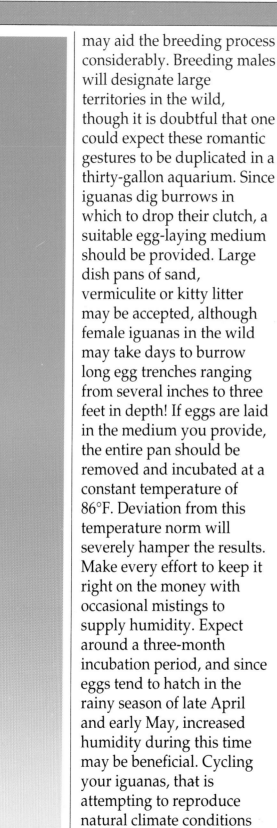

may aid the breeding process considerably. Breeding males will designate large territories in the wild, though it is doubtful that one could expect these romantic gestures to be duplicated in a thirty-gallon aquarium. Since iguanas dig burrows in which to drop their clutch, a suitable egg-laying medium should be provided. Large dish pans of sand, vermiculite or kitty litter may be accepted, although female iguanas in the wild may take days to burrow long egg trenches ranging from several inches to three feet in depth! If eggs are laid in the medium you provide, the entire pan should be removed and incubated at a constant temperature of 86°F. Deviation from this temperature norm will severely hamper the results. Make every effort to keep it right on the money with occasional mistings to supply humidity. Expect around a three-month incubation period, and since eggs tend to hatch in the rainy season of late April and early May, increased humidity during this time may be beneficial. Cycling your iguanas, that is attempting to reproduce natural climate conditions

for your breeding pair, may or may not increase your chances for success. Many reptile breeders painstakingly study the environment from which their pets have been plucked and go to lengths trying to duplicate these seasonal changes for captives. The process should entail a

The American tropics contain many moderately large iguanid lizards that are seldom kept as pets for various reasons. This is *Plica plica* from South America, an attractive species that is seldom imported.

cooling down procedure of gently lowering temperatures combined with shorter "days" (a simple timer attached to your cage's lighting system can handle this task) to imitate the winter season. At this time, the male and female specimens are generally kept separately. To recreate springtime, light cycles are increased, accompanied by corresponding increases in the cage temperature; following this procedure, the males and females are introduced and breeding should occur. It should be pointed out, however, that this scientific process has its drawbacks. It may take

Large iguanas can be a handful. If you allow them to exercise outside, keep them under constant supervision to prevent escapes. If you handle a large iguana, be sure to provide some support for the rear end of the body and the tail.

which part of the world it has been transplanted. Since reptile breeding is far from an exact science, it is probably best to employ as much control as possible over the situation (i.e., cycling) instead of leaving it to chance. Hopefully, these calculated efforts to perfect the art of reptile breeding will result in successful programs not only to supply the pet trade but to replenish populations in the wild.

considerable research to establish the exact climatic conditions optimum for the particular race or subspecies of lizard that you are attempting to breed. Other successful breeders of reptiles report equally adequate results by simply housing pairs or colonies of animals together year 'round and letting Nature take her course. A South American species, for example, will tend to get spring fever at the same time each year, corresponding with the breeding season in its homeland, no matter to

Many smaller desert-dwelling iguanids make poor pets and should not be taken from the wild. One example is the horned lizards, *Phrynosoma*, which have very strict temperature and humidity requirements (high and very low, respectively) and feed mostly on ants.

THE FUTURE OF THE IGUANA

The Green Iguana has always been quite efficient at propagating its species, as evidenced by the large numbers seen in the wild, the many thousands imported to fuel the pet trade, the many sold in markets of Latin America as food, as well as the great number shipped to schools and biological supply houses for study and dissection. In recent years, however, the gross number of iguanas in the wild has diminished sharply and should be viewed as cause for our concern. The aforementioned excesses have undoubtedly taken their toll to some extent, although the principal threat to the remaining population is the destruction of their natural breeding grounds. As civilization presses onward, more and more areas of virgin tundra and rain forest are irrevocably altered to accommodate man. The Green Iguana may soon face the situation which has caused so many species of animals and plants to become scarce or extinct; its population being over-collected combined with the destruction of the habitat in which it must propagate. It is likely that this situation will

be arrested before the iguana joins its numerous extinct reptilian relatives in the history books; however, it does require immediate attention from pet owners, breeders and importers, as well as protective legislation in Latin America. It is never too early to enforce conservation, although in many unfortunate cases it has been too late.

Holbrookia maculata lacks an eardrum that is visible externally, so it often is called an earless lizard. Actually, the inner ear is well developed. The lizard can sense movement through vibrations of the sand better than it can hear air-borne sounds, however.

An Antillean
Iguana in its
natural habitat.

INDEX

PHOTO CREDITS:
William B. Allen, Jr., Dr. Herbert R. Axelrod, R.D. Bartlett, Michael Cardwell, J. Dommers, Dodd, Shelly K. Ferrell, Lyle Flesher, Isabelle Francais, Dr. Fredric Fry (from the *Reptile Care* book), Michael Gilroy, J. Harris, B. Kahl, R.J. Koestler, Ken Lucas— Courtesy of Steinhart Aquarium, Anita Malhotra, David R. Moenich, K.T. Nemuras, John R. Quinn, R.G. Sprackland, K.H. Switak, Tidbits Studio, R. Allen Winstel.